Helen Williamson

A FARMER'S ALPHABET

A FARMER'S ALPHABET

MARY AZARIAN

DAVID R. GODINE✦PUBLISHER
✦BOSTON✦

First published in 1981 by
David R. Godine, Publisher, Inc.
306 Dartmouth Street
Boston, Massachusetts 02116

ISBN 0-87923-394-X (hardcover)
ISBN 0-87923-397-4 (softcover)
LC 80-84938

Designed by Hal Morgan

Third printing, November 1981

Printed in the United States of America

Bb

Barn

Dd

Dog

Ee

Eggs

Hh

1865

Horse

I i

Icicles

Nn

Neighbor

Quilt

Rr

Rocker

S s

Stove

Tt

Toad

Artist's Note

THE IDEA of doing an alphabet related to rural themes grew during my years as a teacher in a one-room school in northern Vermont. Arriving for my first day of teaching, I found the large schoolroom entirely bare, except for the wooden desks. An inspection of the various cupboards and shelves revealed only a scattering of old textbooks. The need for warmth, light, and color was obvious, and my first project was to make a set of alphabet posters that almost encircled the room. This was the beginning of a fascination with alphabet images that has stayed with me long after my teaching days ended.

I began designing *A Farmer's Alphabet* with the idea of creating a decorative teaching aid that would celebrate some of the rural traditions that still are observed in New England today. I grew up on a small Virginia farm and watched while it and the surrounding countryside were slowly flattened into an asphalt suburbia, a depressing process to observe and one that is being repeated across rural America at an ever-quickening pace. I wanted to make an alphabet to replace the many urban-oriented ones already available, and thus help in the fight to maintain regional diversity. The idea of hundreds of farm and village children learning that "M is for MacDonalds" or "S is for Shopping Mall," and that such signs of "progress" are both desirable and inevitable, dismayed me. It is sad that traditions are valued only after they are lost. In my own alphabet, "M" would be for "Maple Syrup," in recognition of an important springtime activity on many small farms, and "S" would be represented by "Stove," one of those big black woodburning cook-stoves that still warm many rural kitchens. In choosing each image, I tried to avoid quaintness and concentrated instead on activities or objects of proven practicality and relevance to modern life. Fortunately, Vermont's Department of Education approved of my plans and decided to have enough sets printed to supply every elementary school in Vermont.

Each alphabet poster was done as a woodcut. The woodcut is one of the oldest methods of making a picture that can be reproduced many times. It is a simple craft, requiring only a piece of suitable wood, a set of good quality woodcut knives, ink, and paper on which to print the finished carving. A design is drawn directly onto a piece of smooth straight-grained wood, and one must always remember that the printed image will be the reverse of the drawing on the block. Letters must be carefully drawn backwards or the printed words will be unreadable.

THIS IS BACKWARDS

After the drawing is completed, all areas of the wood block *not drawn on* are

cut away, leaving the original image in the form of raised ridges. The block is then inked with a roller, or brayer, and a piece of special handmade rice paper is carefully laid on the inked block. The woodcut is printed by rubbing on the paper with a smooth wooden dowel or a wooden spoon. This transfers the image from the block to the paper. It is essential not to move the paper while printing or the printed image will be distorted. The finished print is then hung up to dry for a day or so. Many prints can be made from one block, and presses are sometimes used to print woodcuts in larger quantities.

Every artist has his or her own favorite medium of work. Although I have done both painting and drawing, woodcutting remains for me the most exciting form of expression. I occasionally work in maple or cherry, but prefer basswood, some of which comes from the woodlot of our hillside farm. I feel very fortunate to have been able to make a profession of doing woodcuts in a still beautiful rural area.

A FARMER'S ALPHABET
has been set in Cheltenham Old Style by Typographic House of
Boston, Massachusetts. The Cheltenham family of faces,
designed by Bertram G. Goodhue for Ingalls Kimball of the
Cheltenham Press of New York, was offered in the catalogues of
the American Type Founders in twelve variations.
An immediate success, it combined the obvious virtues of
legibility and printability with overtones of Art Nouveau and
William Morris. In the first twenty years of this century
Cheltenham was used more widely for both book and advertising
work than any other type in America. The paper is
Monadnock Text, an entirely acid-free laid sheet. The book
has been printed offset and bound by Book Press
of Brattleboro, Vermont.